INSIDER INFORMATION

What Wall Street Doesn't Want
Your Street to Know

WILLIAM A. EADDY II

Copyright © 2024 William A. Eaddy II
All rights reserved
First Edition

PAGE PUBLISHING
Conneaut Lake, PA

First originally published by Page Publishing 2024

ISBN 978-1-64628-207-4 (pbk)
ISBN 978-1-64628-208-1 (digital)

Printed in the United States of America

DEDICATION

This book is dedicated to my stunning and beautiful wife, Sharice Eaddy. Thank you for your love, support, friendship, and partnership on this journey of life. You motivate me and hold me accountable to become the very best version of myself and to live out the gifts and talents that God has placed within. I'll love you beyond eternity.

ACKNOWLEDGMENTS

To my daughters and bonuses—Clarke, Essence, Essasia, Ryan, and Ellanah; parents—Dr. Michael and Christine Rose Eaddy; siblings—Renee Pegues, Ephraim Eaddy, and Eunice Eaddy; nieces and nephews—Caleb James Huff, Amir Pegues, Elizabeth Eaddy, Joanna Eaddy, Moriah Eaddy, and Faith Eaddy. I love and appreciate you.

To Rita Harris, James Gilliam, Irene Baker, Bill Fanter, Tim Pieropoulos, and Steve Williams, my mentors in banking who developed within me the knowledge, confidence, and ability to lead at the highest levels for two of the country's largest financial institutions. Thank you.

To the People's Church of the Harvest COGIC, friends, family, associates, and the community that supports me, thank you.

In memory of my grandmother, Jessie Shields, and cousin, Sharonda Burnett. Fly high, my angels.

CONTENTS

Dedication 3
Acknowledgments 5

Chapter 1 9
Chapter 1:   The Accounts Banks Offer 9
Chapter 2:   The Purpose of Convenience Products 20
Chapter 3:   The Purpose of Credit Products 24
Chapter 4:   Personal Attention to Address Individual Needs 30
Chapter 5:   The Banks' Purpose for the Accounts 38
Chapter 6:   The Truth about "Convenience" 44
Chapter 7:   The Truth about Loans 51
Chapter 8:   What's Really Motivating the Bankers,
             Tellers, and Managers 56
Chapter 9:   The Pressure to Impress Wall Street 62
Chapter 10: Who It's Really about—the Shareholders 69

CHAPTER 1

The Accounts Banks Offer

I would like to begin this book by saying that my fifteen-plus years in banking have been a rollercoaster of a ride with many great, thrilling, exciting, mind-blowing ups that were filled with some deep, stomach-turning twists and downs. Overall, the banking world has taught me some of the most valuable lessons that I could have ever learned concerning business, and thanks in part to that education and experience, I gladly welcome you into the wealth of knowledge that my career provided.

I would like to ask you a question, Why do we use banks? A couple of different answers come into my mind:

- I use the bank so that I don't have to keep cash on hand.
- I use the bank so that I'm not keeping cash in an unsafe place such as under my mattress or in a safe within my house that could potentially be broken into and stolen.
- I use the bank so that I can have records reflecting all of my deposits made.
- I use the bank so that I can have records reflecting all withdrawals and purchases made.

Do we share some of the same thoughts and reasons? Most likely so or probably not very different or far off. With that now established and understood, let us discuss the different types of accounts banks offer and the benefits available to you.

This may seem elementary for many, but just as a quick refresher, let us talk about some of the accounts offered by banks, but first, let us define the word *account*.

Account. (1) An amount of money deposited with a bank, as in a checking or savings account. (2) A statement of financial transactions. (3) A formal record of the debits and credits relating to the person, business, etc., named at the head of the ledger account. (4) A balance of a specified period's receipts and expenditures. (5) A business relation in which credit is used. (6) Any customer or client, esp. one carried on a regular credit basis.

The Checking Account

Practically everyone has a checking account with some financial institution, whether that is a bank or savings and loan association. Even high school teenagers can open what is commonly referred to as "student checking" at most institutions. Most banks do require that a minor list a parent or guardian on the account as well, although there are some instances where that is not necessary. However, I do caution parents and guardians to assess the maturity and level of responsibility their child possesses *before* allowing them to own a checking account.

The checking account's primary function is for individuals to deposit funds into it in order to make withdrawals and purchases with a draft instrument that we commonly refer to as a "check." Banks typically provide customers with a check register that will serve as a record-keeping document of all deposits and withdrawals, including purchases made. (I am sure that someone is saying, *Check register? Are you serious, Will? There is something called online banking that exists.* Trust me, we will discuss that resource a little later in the book.) Either way, understand that it is your responsibility to maintain accurate records of all of your account transactions.

It is also the requirement of every institution and banker that you do business with to provide you with documentation such as

Account Rules and Regulations, which clearly explain the expectations of the bank concerning the handling of your account. This document educates you, the customer, of the *Do's and Don'ts* as it pertains to the account. This document may seem lengthy and filled with a lot of jargon that you just do not feel like reading. However, it is in your best interest to familiarize yourself with what is expected and required by the bank in order to keep your account in good standing and avoid any penalties or fees for violating the rules and regulations.

Banks offer checking accounts that do not require keeping a minimum balance of monies in the account at all times. The benefit of this zero balance account is that your money is 100 percent available to you for your use. There are also checking accounts that do require a minimum balance, and in this case, the bank typically will pay you, the customer, interest on the funds within the account as long as that minimum balance is maintained. The benefit of minimum balance requirement accounts is that it helps to discipline you in keeping money in your account at all times.

The Savings Account

The savings account has a primary function of doing just what its name says—*saving* your money. The savings account typically requires that a minimum balance be maintained (ballpark figure of $250). The bank agrees to pay you interest (i.e., today's rates of 0.10 percent annual percentage yield (APY) on balances ranging from $0 to $25,000) on those funds for maintaining the minimum balance requirement. The bank also may pay more interest in tiers as it relates to the higher balances that you keep in the account. The benefit to you is this: as you continue to discipline yourself to save more money, the more money you will earn.

In this day and age (especially considering where we are presently as a country), as it pertains to the economy and job losses, etc., everyone should do their very best now to save and put money aside in case of any rainy or more likely, thunderous, dark, and windy days. Savings accounts are just one of the many vehicles banks offer to people who have the mindset to save and accumulate interest.

Money Market Accounts

Money market accounts are another savings vehicle offered to the public by financial institutions. Money market accounts work, for the most part, exactly the same way that a savings account does. The difference is that it requires a higher minimum balance (ballpark figure of $1,000) to be maintained within the account in order to earn interest on those funds (i.e., today's rates of 0.05 to 0.85 percent tiered on balances from $0 to 500,000 plus).

Because it requires a higher balance, the benefit of having a money market account is that it helps customers discipline themselves to always maintain a certain amount of money in their account, thus in most cases, earning them a higher return of interest than that of a savings account.

Certificate of Deposit

Certificate of deposit, commonly referred to as a CD, is yet another savings vehicle offered to the public by financial institutions. The primary function of a CD is to require that customers enter into an agreement with the bank to place a specific amount (typical minimum balance requirement of $1,000) into an account that the customer agrees not to touch for a specified amount of time (periods vary from three months to sixty months). In return for depositing the money into the CD for the agreed-upon time frame, the bank will pay interest to the customer on those funds (i.e., today's rates of 1.98 to 3.25 percent APY) in tiers depending on the balance maintained.

The benefit again to you, the customer, is that you will generally receive a higher interest rate on CDs with longer terms and higher balances.

The Safety of the Checking, Savings, Money Market, and Certificate of Deposit Accounts

Each one of these accounts is completely safe to have without any risk of loss except if the financial institution happens to go out of

INSIDER INFORMATION

business. Even in the unfortunate event of a bank failure (i.e., no longer having the capacity to lend or return the funds deposited to their customers), there is what is known as FDIC Insurance that protects customers up to a certain amount (currently $250,000). In order to better understand how many accounts you can have covered under this insurance provided by financial institutions, you must read that little book that I referred to at the beginning of this chapter entitled *Account Rules and Regulations*. I told you that you need to take time to familiarize yourself with that information, didn't I?

For those wondering what FDIC means exactly, here is a clearer explanation as per *Wikipedia*:

> The Federal Deposit Insurance Corporation (FDIC) is a United States government corporation created by the Glass-Steagall Act of 1933. It provides deposit insurance, which guarantees the safety of deposits in member banks, currently up to $250,000 per depositor per bank. The FDIC insures deposits at 8,195 institutions. The FDIC also examines and supervises certain financial institutions for safety and soundness, performs certain consumer-protection functions, and manages banks in receiverships (failed banks).

Insured institutions are required to place signs at their place of business stating that "deposits are backed by the full faith and credit of the United States Government." Since the start of FDIC Insurance on January 1, 1934, no depositor has lost a single cent of insured funds because of a bank failure. Therefore, you can rest assured that your money is safe in whatever financial institution you choose to do business with when it comes to holding these specific accounts.

Having been a licensed investment adviser for over ten years, I thoroughly enjoyed advising, teaching, and assisting people and businesses to accomplish their financial goals and objectives. What I found to be so fascinating and intriguing, as it related to advising people with investments, was the fact that individual and business banking need to each have their own DNA and identity. What I mean very plainly is that no one is the same; everyone is different no matter how alike two people or businesses may be.

In the same manner that every person and every business has its own identity, they also have different things that are important to them, and they prefer different ways of ultimately getting where they desire to be financially. When it comes to investing, there is no one-size-fits-all approach. If ever you have asked or heard anyone say, *I know just the perfect thing for you to invest in,* before they sat down with you and asked specific questions to determine what is best for your situation, please allow me to advise you to run as fast as you can in the opposite direction of that financial idiot!

If you come across anyone using that approach, please understand that they do not care one thing about you, your hard-earned money, goals, dreams, or objectives. I, unfortunately, have worked with and known people that have operated this way, and it cost people a lot, if not everything. In my book *All You Need to Know and Understand about Investing,* I talk more specifically about what that experience *should* be like between you and your adviser.

With that being said, let's discuss just a few investment vehicles offered by financial institutions and investment companies. But first, let's get a better understanding of what the words *investment* and *stocks* mean.

Investment. (1) The investing of money or capital in order to gain profitable returns as interest, income, or appreciation in value. (2) A thing invested in, as a business, a quantity of shares of stock, etc. (3) Property or another possession acquired for future financial return or benefit.

Stocks. (1) The outstanding capital of a company or corporation. (2) The shares of a particular company or corporation. (3) The certificate of ownership of such stock; stock certificate.

Stocks are one of many vehicles that financial institutions offer to help individuals earn both interest and income on money invested. The purpose of stock is to essentially *grow* your money. As a licensed financial adviser, it was imperative to find out exactly what the client wanted to accomplish, what their time line was in order to accomplish their financial objective, and what their risk tolerance was.

These are all very important because the answers to these questions, along with many others, help to identify exactly what the most suitable and appropriate recommendation should be for a client. You must keep in mind when dealing with stock that there is significant *risk* involved where the potential for loss of money is very real. However, with the same exact level of risk involved, there is a significant opportunity for *reward*.

Bonds. (1) A certificate of ownership of a specified portion of a debt due to be paid by a government or corporation to an individual holder and usually bearing a fixed rate of interest. (2) The money deposited or the promissory arrangement entered into under any such agreement. (3) A certificate of debt issued by a government or corporation guaranteeing payment of the original investment, plus interest by a specified future date.

Bonds actually work in a similar manner to that of a CD. As previously discussed, with a CD, you agree to lend the bank your money for a specific period of time and an agreed-upon return of interest. The difference is that instead of just lending to the bank, you now also lend your money to the federal government or a corporation.

Mutual Fund. An investment company that continually offers new shares and buys existing shares back at the request of the shareholder and uses its capital to invest in diversified securities of other companies.

Mutual funds better suit the moderately aggressive investor who wants the reward of investing in the stock market with less risk than owning a specific stock possesses. Although there is risk associated with owning mutual funds, look at it this way: if someone happened to throw a rock through a window with six square panes, there would certainly be damage to fix. But some investors would much rather replace two of the squares instead of the entire window. The same theory applies with mutual funds—if the market takes a dip, there may be loss depending on what is inside of the mutual fund but not as much had all of the money been placed into one specific stock.

One of the many ways to identify what type of investor you are is by asking yourself, "If the market went down 20 percent, and I had all of my money (i.e., $10,000) invested into just one stock, what would I do?" Whereas with a mutual fund, based on the customer(s) financial objective, if the market went down 20 percent, yes, there would likely be some loss, however, if that same mutual fund had bonds in it, there would also be financial gains to enjoy. Why? Because when stocks do not perform well, bonds do, and vice versa. This is referred to as an inverse relationship. Again, these important topics are covered in *All You Need to Know and Understand About Investing*.

Financial institutions offer many different types of accounts for you to take advantage of the varied benefits that they offer. It is your responsibility to not only educate yourself but identify a trustworthy individual that can help you to better understand all of the ins and outs of these relationships.

What you must first understand is that an investment is not guaranteed to make you money. However, in the same manner that FDIC Insurance covers deposits, investments are covered by SIPC Insurance. Let's discuss what exactly SIPC is as explained by the SIPC Insurance website below:

SIPC and Other Account Insurance

TradeStar Investments Inc. is a member of SIPC, which protects securities of customers of its members up to $500,000 (including $100,000 for claims of cash). An explanatory brochure is available upon request or at www.sipc.org. Additional coverage is provided through a highly regarded insurer on accounts that are held at our clearing firm, Fiserv Securities Inc., member SIPC/NYSE/NASD. Both SIPC and the additional coverage provides protection in the event of a member firm failure and do not insure against market decline.

INSIDER INFORMATION

What SIPC Covers...and What It Does Not

SIPC is *not* the FDIC. The Securities Investor Protection Corporation does not offer to investors the same blanket protection that the Federal Deposit Insurance Corporation provides to bank depositors.

How are SIPC and the FDIC different? When a member bank fails, the FDIC insures all depositors at that institution against loss up to a certain dollar limit. The FDIC's no-questions-asked approach makes sense because the banking world is "risk averse." Most savers put their money in FDIC-insured bank accounts because they can't afford to lose their money.

That is *precisely* the opposite of how investors behave in the stock market, in which rewards are only possible with risk. Most market losses are a normal part of the ups and downs of the risk-oriented world of investing. That is why SIPC does not bail out investors when the value of their stocks, bonds, and other investments fall for any reason. Instead, SIPC replaces missing stocks and other securities where it is possible to do so even when investments have increased in value.

SIPC does not cover individuals who are sold worthless stocks and other securities. SIPC helps individuals whose money, stocks, and other securities are stolen by a broker or put at risk when a brokerage fails for other reasons.

How We Help

What You Need to Know about SIPC

Understanding the rules is the key to protecting yourself...and your money.

1. *When SIPC gets involved.* When a brokerage firm fails, SIPC usually asks a federal court to appoint a trustee to liquidate the firm and protect its customers. With smaller

brokerage firm failures, SIPC sometimes deals directly with customers.

2. *Investors eligible for SIPC help.* SIPC aids most customers of failed brokerage firms. (A list of ineligible investors may be found in the fourth question in the next section of this brochure.)

3. *Investments protected by SIPC.* The cash and securities—such as stocks and bonds—held by a customer at a financially troubled brokerage firm are protected by SIPC. Among the investments that are *ineligible* for SIPC protections are commodity futures contracts, fixed annuity contracts, and currency, as well as investment contracts (such as limited partnerships) that are not registered with the U.S. Securities and Exchange Commission under the Securities Act of 1933.

4. *Terms of SIPC help.* Customers of a failed brokerage firm get back all securities (such as stocks and bonds) that already are registered in their name or are in the process of being registered. After this first step, the firm's remaining customer assets are then divided on a pro rata basis with funds shared in proportion to the size of claims. If sufficient funds are not available in the firm's customer accounts to satisfy claims within these limits, the reserve funds of SIPC are used to supplement the distribution, up to a ceiling of $500,000 per customer, including a maximum of $100,000 for cash claims. Additional funds may be available to satisfy the remainder of customer claims after the cost of liquidating the brokerage firm is taken into account.

5. *How account transfers work.* In a failed brokerage firm with accurate records, the court-appointed trustee and SIPC may arrange to have some or all customer accounts transferred to another brokerage firm. Customers whose accounts are transferred are notified promptly and then have the option of staying at the new firm or moving to another brokerage of their choosing.

6. *How claims are valued.* Typically, when SIPC asks a court to put a troubled brokerage firm in liquidation, the financial worth of a customer's account is calculated as of the "filing date." Wherever possible, the actual stocks and other securities owned by a customer are returned to him or her. To accomplish this, SIPC's reserve funds will be used, if necessary, to purchase replacement securities (such as stocks) in the open market. It is always possible that market changes or fraud at the failed brokerage firm (or elsewhere) will result in the returned securities having lost some—or even all—of their value. In other cases, the securities may have increased in value.

The Role of SIPC

SIPC is your first line of defense in the event of a brokerage firm failure. No fewer than 99 percent of eligible investors get their investments back from SIPC. From its creation by Congress in 1970 through December 2001, SIPC advanced $513 million in order to make possible the recovery of $13.9 billion in assets for an estimated 622,000 investors.

When a brokerage is closed due to bankruptcy or other financial difficulties, the Securities Investor Protection Corporation steps in as quickly as possible and, within certain limits, works to return to you cash, stock, and other securities you had at the firm. Without SIPC, investors at financially troubled brokerage firms might lose their securities or money forever...or wait for years while their assets are tied up in court.

CHAPTER 2

The Purpose of Convenience Products

We live in such a fast-paced environment that most people want access to their cash and their account information within a New York minute. Thanks to the technological advances that have been provided over the last twenty years, customers can access their information almost that fast.

Along with the plethora of accounts that financial institutions offer comes what is commonly referred to as "convenience products" that serve the purpose of giving its customers access to their account relationships whenever they would like that information. Some of the convenience products that banks offer are ATM debit/credit cards, checks, online banking, and online bill pay.

ATM Debit/Credit Cards. A plastic card that resembles a credit card but functions like a check, and through which, payments for purchases or services are made electronically to the bank accounts of participating retail establishments directly from those of cardholders.

ATM debit/credit cards offer many benefits such as keeping you from carrying large amounts of cash on your person. Losing hard-earned cash under any circumstance is not a good feeling because we all know that once the cash is gone, it is in fact, gone.

Owning an ATM debit/credit card provides the convenience of making purchases simply by swiping your card and entering in a secret personal identification number (PIN) code, which only you should know. While we are on the topic, please do everything within your power to keep your PIN confidential, and do not use anything too easy such as your birthday, the last four numbers of your social security number, or anything someone who may find your card could figure out.

Again, I want you to understand that it is your responsibility to safeguard your personal information. I cannot begin to explain to you the countless number of times that someone has had his or her exact PIN inside of a purse or wallet along with their ATM debit/credit card. Although you were not the individual that actually made the withdrawal, in this scenario, you are still overall responsible for the negligence in doing your part to protect your account from fraud.

Unfortunately, when this happens, it is highly unlikely that you will be able to prove that you did not make the withdrawal or place yourself in a compromising situation that clearly could have been avoided. With that being the case, the likelihood of those transactions or fees being reversed is very low. Again, this only applies to transactions performed at an ATM using your very own secure PIN.

Now I also want to clarify the fact that although it is called an ATM debit/credit card, the funds are directly tied to the balance within your checking account. You have a choice of how you want to have your transaction processed, either as a debit or a credit. The only difference between the two functions is that, with a debit card, you are required to enter your confidential PIN in order to complete the transaction. Processing the transaction as a credit requires a signature in order to complete it. Regardless of how you choose to have the transaction processed and completed, all of the funds are coming directly out of your checking account. There is no line of credit that this particular card is linked to.

Check. A written order, usually on a standard printed form, directing a bank to pay money.

Before the introduction of the ATM debit/credit card, a check was the most commonly used instrument in transacting business other than just using cash. Checks enable you to purchase goods or pay for services rendered by using a paper instrument that has your name, address, bank account, and routing number along with the number of the check. The check specifies who it is made payable to and the exact dollar amount to be paid.

Online Banking

Online banking is a convenience product that records all transactions that have already posted and are currently pending on your account. The benefit of online banking is that, typically, it is a free service that records all purchases, withdrawals, and deposits.

Having this feature on your account also helps to save customers money by allowing them to monitor their account balances and make funds transfers in real time from other accounts in order to avoid overdraft fees by covering pending transactions, which may have exceeded the customer's available balance.

Usually at little or no cost, online banking offers customers the convenience of printing copies of their statements and canceled checks—just point and click, and you have what you need at your fingertips. Of course, each financial institution is different, but you can typically go back six months or even as far back as one year to receive printouts of your checks and statements.

Online banking also helps customers to detect and fight against fraud because most every transaction that posts to your account happens immediately. The faster that a customer can recognize fraud on their account, the faster they can alert the bank in order to minimize the damages and initiate an investigation to protect the customer, the bank, and hopefully, identify the perpetrator.

Clearly, online banking has many benefits for customers. It is my recommendation that every customer utilize this resource to the best of their ability. Using online banking in conjunction with your check register will aid in making sure your account balance is accurate.

Online Bill Pay

Online bill pay is a tool that allows customers to schedule and pay bills when they want to. Many companies that customers do frequent business with receive the payments on the day that the customer selects and thus provide electronic versions of the payment received on the customer's monthly banking statement at no cost.

Since the customer must pay to purchase blank checks after the ones initially provided by the bank are depleted, this feature also saves the customer that cost. Online bill pay also saves the money spent on stamps and envelopes used to mail payments.

Lastly, online bill pay conveniently allows the customer to just point and click in order to handle their personal business rather than spending time writing out checks, filling and sealing envelopes, and then delivering the payments to the mailbox or post office.

Safety of Online Banking and Bill Pay

Throughout my fifteen years of banking, I have never seen an individual's information compromised by someone hacking into the banks' systems. All of the financial institutions that I have worked for have done an incredible job protecting the privacy of its customers.

Many customers find themselves fearful and reluctant to send their personal information over the airwaves of computers. I would like to encourage each of you to utilize these resources because it is absolutely safe. And on the off chance that someone successfully hacks into a bank's computer systems and accesses your personal information, always remember that the first place any transactions will be reflected is on your statement in online banking.

CHAPTER 3

The Purpose of Credit Products

Financial institutions assist literally millions of customers in acquiring major purchases through credit products such as personal secured and unsecured loans, personal lines of credit, home equity loans, home equity lines of credit, refinances, and personal secured and unsecured credit cards, just to name a few. Before we discuss each product in depth, for educational purposes, let's define exactly what *credit* means.

Credit. (1) Confidence in a purchaser's ability and intention to pay, displayed by entrusting the buyer with goods or services without immediate payment. (2) Reputation of solvency and probity, entitling a person to be trusted in buying or borrowing.

In essence, financial institutions extend credit to consumers to provide the funds needed in the form of a loan based on certain factors (underwriting) to determine the likelihood of the loan being repaid with interest without interruption. Now let's take a look at the different credit products that financial institutions offer and how you, the customer, benefit from them.

Personal Secured Loans

A personal secured loan is a loan extended by the bank that is guaranteed by the customer with his/her own funds. For example, let's say you want to purchase a car and had disciplined yourself to save a down payment of $15,000. Instead of paying cash for the vehicle, you could place that $15,000 into a CD for whatever terms you agree upon in order to secure (guarantee) the loan. By doing this, you accomplish a couple of things:

- You preserve the money that you worked hard to save.
- You earn interest on those funds during the agreed-upon term.
- You usually will pay a lower interest rate than that of a standard unsecured loan.
- If, for whatever reason, you can no longer make the payment, you already have the funds to pay the vehicle off available in the CD.
- You build your credit rating every month that you make your payment on time just as you would have if you made payments on an unsecured loan.
- Once the balance is completely paid off (without interruption), you have the amount you started with plus interest free and clear.

The benefit of this type of loan is that it does not involve much risk to you or the bank. I would typically recommend this product to customers who need to make large withdrawals to purchase or pay off something, yet were not approved for an unsecured loan due to credit issues, etc. Throughout my banking career, I discovered most customers had no clue that such products or options even existed.

Personal Unsecured Loan

Personal unsecured loans are based primarily on one's credit, income, length of time on the job, etc. This type of loan requires underwriters to take a thorough look at these factors and objectively make approval decisions that are in the best interest of the financial institution and the customer's ability to repay without default.

Most unsecured loans range from $0 to $10,000 at an interest rate that can vary based on the customer's credit rating, and as we all know, the better your credit, the better your rate. Once approved, the funds are disbursed by check or direct deposited into the customer's account of choice. Finally, the monthly bill arrives for payment.

The benefits of a personal unsecured loan are the following:

- You borrow the bank's money based on passing the underwriting criteria without having to secure your own funds.
- You build and strengthen your credit as you pay your bills on time.
- You establish history with a financial institution that you may need to borrow larger amounts from in the future.

Personal Lines of Credit

A personal line of credit works almost identically as a personal loan. The only difference between the two is that a personal line of credit does not require that the loan proceeds be immediately disbursed to the customer. Rather, the funds are available for the customer to use anytime.

A customer can actually use the funds for whatever purpose they desire whether it is to pay bills, make a purchase, or just allow the funds to sit in an account. The choice is completely left to them. Customers benefit from a couple of things as it relates to personal lines of credit:

- Easy access to funds when needed.
- No interest to pay when the line has not been advanced.
- Only pay interest on the outstanding balance.
- Variable low-interest rates typically lower than prime rates that move with the market, which benefits the customer.
- As the loan balance is paid back, the money becomes available again without the customer having to reapply for another loan.

INSIDER INFORMATION

Home Equity Loans and Lines of Credit

Before we talk about home equity loans and lines of credit, please allow me to define what equity is.

Equity. (1) The monetary value of a property or business beyond any amounts owed on it in mortgages, claims, liens, etc. (2) Ownership, esp. when considered as the right to share in future profits or appreciation in value. (3) In real estate, the financial value of someone's property over and above the amount the person owes on mortgages.

Allow me to provide you with a hypothetical example:

If you purchased your home for $180,000 at 6 percent for thirty years and put down $20,000 for your down payment, after ten years of making timely payments of $959.28, the balance on the house would be $133,897. The equity in the home that is free and clear of any liens would equal $46,103.

The equity amount of $46,103 is what you can borrow against up to generally 80 percent. Although some financial institutions will go as far as 100 percent loan to value (LTV). In this scenario, the same rules apply whether you take out a loan or open a line of credit.

When a customer applies for a home equity loan, the same personal underwriting criteria apply, along with an appraisal of the value of the home. Once approved, the customer will receive a disbursement of the funds based on the reason stated during the application process for the loan. For example, if you applied for a home equity loan, and you stated that the funds would be used to pay off your car and credit cards, then that is exactly who those checks would be made payable to for the amounts given.

In the scenario of a customer applying for a home equity line of credit, those funds again can be utilized for whatever purpose the customer chooses whether that be to make purchases, pay off debt, or elect not to use the funds at all, and allow it to just remain open as a line of credit. The choice of when and how to use those funds is left to the discretion of the customer.

Refinances

As time passes on, everything changes, including the economy and the interest rates for loans. Whether rates increase or decrease and depending on individual and specific need(s), refinance is another tool that customers can use to their advantage. Let's define refinance.

Refinance. (1) To finance again. (2) To satisfy (a debt) by making another loan on new terms. (3) To increase or change the financing of, as by selling stock or obtaining additional credit. (4) To provide new financing or new financing for, as by discharging a mortgage with the proceeds from a new mortgage obtained at a lower interest rate. (5) To renew or reorganize the financing of. (6) To revise the terms of (a debt obligation) esp. in regard to interest rate or payment schedule. (7) To finance something anew. (8) To extend the maturity of a loan. (9) When a business or person revises their payment schedule for repaying debt. (10) Replacing an older loan with a new loan offering better terms.

With a thorough understanding of the meaning of refinancing, let's use the following example to show the benefit of this type of lending product:

Here is an example: A married couple purchased a home ten years ago for $200,000 at an interest rate of 8.5 percent. The monthly payment for that original mortgage is $1,537.83. After ten years of making their payments, the remaining balance would be $177,205.09. Well, as we all know, rates have dropped dramatically below 8.5 percent over the past ten years.

The couple decides to refinance the remaining balance of $177,205.83 at a lower rate of 5.5 percent for the remaining twenty years. The monthly mortgage payment for the same period of time is now $1,218.98, a monthly savings of $318.85 or $3826.20 annually or $76,524 over twenty years.

Now *that* is the power of refinancing! Can you imagine what opportunity would be lost to customers without this great lending tool? Seventy-six thousand five hundred twenty-four dollars is the least that would have been lost. But imagine the potential loss of return on that $76,524 had it been placed into an investment to save for retirement, college expenses, etc.

Personal Secured/Unsecured Credit Cards

Credit cards are offered by financial institutions to benefit customers in the exact same manner that a personal secured or unsecured line of credit does. The only difference is that a customer accesses the funds through making purchases with the card or performing cash advances to receive the cash available on the card.

A number of benefits to having a credit card are the following:

- You use (borrow) the money on the card from the financial institution that approved you without using your own funds to make purchases.
- You only pay interest on the amount that you use.
- The available balance is made available to you over and over as you continuously repay without having to reapply.
- You build credit history with the card provider.

Credit cards require approval of underwriting criteria, which include credit history, time on the job, salary, etc.

Secured credit cards work the same way that a secured loan works *except* that a line of credit is established using your own personal funds. The amount can vary from bank to bank; however, it is usually a ballpark figure of $300 to establish a secured credit card. Although the card is secured, it works in the exact same way that a regular credit card does.

We have covered a number of different credit products offered by financial institutions all over the world. Throughout my career, I have always tried to educate and inform clients of the resources available to them through various loans and lines of credit. I have proudly helped literally thousands of clients and customers save a lot of money with these very same products.

CHAPTER 4

Personal Attention to Address Individual Needs

I have great respect for the fine people that serve as branch managers, bankers, and tellers. Having built my career in financial institutions by serving in every capacity—from teller to manager—gives me a unique understanding of both customer and client expectations.

When customers enter the branch, they expect to receive friendly, courteous, and prompt service, which is what they rightfully deserve. Financial institutions do everything that they can to identify professional, friendly employees who will to address the needs of their customers. Let's look at the benefits of these three important roles that summarize the personnel of practically every financial institution.

The Tellers

What makes a banking experience either great or miserable nine out of ten times happens right at the teller line. The reason for this is because the teller line experiences the most traffic and has the most transactions performed within the bank.

INSIDER INFORMATION

I will share with you what the expectations of the tellers were at the bank branches that I managed and how they benefit customers:

- *Warmly greet customers within (hopefully) five seconds of their entrance into the branch.*

    How does this benefit customers? First, it lets you know that we acknowledge your presence, and we are not going to act as if we do not notice that you are here. It also hopefully sends the message that *we welcome you and are eager to serve you.* I, myself, as a customer have found that I really look forward to a nice greeting whenever I enter a place of business. Being acknowledged allows me to let my guard down because it at least appears that someone wants to help me.

- *Acknowledge the customer by name at least twice while performing the transaction, preferably at the beginning and at the end.*

    Why use the customer's name? There is nothing like being acknowledged as an individual, and using the customer's name sends a personal message of *we appreciate your business, and it is very important to us.* Important enough that we want to get to know you because we look forward to seeing you in our branch again.

- *Process the customer transaction correctly and efficiently.*

    The last thing any customer wants to have happen is for their transaction to be processed wrong. Most people cannot afford to have numbers transposed that then sets off a chain reaction of errors. Posting the wrong dollar amount may cause other posting items to overdraw the account, thereby incurring customer fees that will have to be reversed.

    In the event the amount entered into the system happens to be more than what it actually is, the same potential problem can occur. In this scenario, the customer may be led to believe that they have more funds in their account than they actually do, which, at some point, will be corrected and again could cause unnecessary fees to be assessed if the customer overspends what they actually should have had in their account.

So please understand that as important as it is for you get in and out of the bank quickly, allow time for the teller to process your transaction correctly. While there are some exceptions to the rule, depending on what all a customer is trying to accomplish, in most cases, it takes no more than five minutes to process the average transaction.

- *Identify possible opportunities to save or make a customer money.*

  Have you ever had a teller ask you about your credit card interest rate or what rate your car or mortgage payment currently is? You probably have. The reason for this is to identify an opportunity to place more money back into your pocket by reducing your current rate on existing credit cards, vehicles, or even your home mortgage.

  Tellers certainly are not trying to be nosy by asking these personal questions. But believe it or not, tellers all over the country have helped millions of customers save lots of money by asking questions that typically take less than a minute to ask and receive an answer. The benefit to you is if there is an opportunity to save or make you money, that simple question was well worth it.

- *Sincerely thank the customer for their business.*

  One of the most important things that a teller can do to solidify a customer having a great experience within the bank is to express sincere thanks. *Nothing says I really appreciate your business like a nice thank you.* It is the last thing that a customer will hear before exiting the bank, so why not send them out feeling appreciated and impressed with the service they received.

These are just a few of the responsibilities most banks expect of tellers (who are directly aligned with customers) to fulfill. Customers may not personally know the manager or the bankers because they typically do not need their services (as far as they know) as often as they utilize teller services.

The Bankers

One of my most enjoyable positions during my career was that of a banker. I really enjoyed helping both customers and clients find the path to meeting their financial goals and objectives. I enjoyed it so much that it is a big part of the reason that I started my own company, the Exclusive Signature Group (ESG). I wanted to incorporate what I most enjoyed back into what it is that I do—working directly face-to-face with the public. Let's discuss some of the expectations that most financial institutions have of bankers, which benefit you, the customer, in the end.

- *Get to know your customer.*

It truly is important for bankers and financial professionals to know their customers. Allow me to explain what "knowing your customer" means. It simply means that your banker or financial professional should have a thorough understanding of what your individual goals and objectives are. Your banker should clearly understand where you are presently and where you ultimately want to go.

Now the only way for your banker to get to know you is to ask questions regarding how you currently do your banking, investing, etc. These are not questions to be nosy but rather to build an understanding of what is already in place and identify the missing pieces to assist you in accomplishing your financial desires.

You, the customer, play the most important part in building a great relationship in order to get where you want to go by honestly answering your banker's questions. I know that there may be someone reading this right now, saying, *Why would I tell a banker everything and answer their questions if I don't really know them?* To answer that question, I recommend that you bank with someone that you trust or ask someone that you have confidence in to find out where he or she does his/her banking. Your honest answers tailor the best recommendations that a financial professional can give. Consider this:

If you go in for a checkup, your doctor will ask you a considerable amount of questions concerning what brought you in to see him/her—questions about

- your personal health,
- the health history of your parents and grandparents,
- current symptoms or pains,
- illnesses, and/or
- allergies.

We all understand that the reason for this process is to help the doctor properly diagnose or make recommendations for continued healthy living. If you do not answer the questions of the doctor openly and honestly, you run the risk of being misdiagnosed. It is imperative to give all pertinent health-related information so that you can recover and/or continue to live healthy.

Apply this very same principle to you and your finances when it comes to dealing with your banker or financial adviser. The more open and honest you are about all of your financial relationships, the better your banker can serve you.

With this being plainly understood now, I would like to ask you a few questions.

- How healthy are you financially?
- When was the last time you were in to see your "financial physician?"
- Are you feeling any financial pains?
- What "exercises" are you doing daily to stay in "financial shape?"
- Do you have a "financially balanced diet?"

As you see, I can go on and on with this analogy. However, my point is that you should view your banker or financial adviser as your "financial physician." In addition, if you do not like (or trust) his/

INSIDER INFORMATION

her advice and/or feel that you can be better served, do your due diligence, and get a second opinion. Overall, make sure you are financially healthy and strong.

To assist you in becoming more comfortable with your banker or financial adviser, let's talk about some of the questions that you may be asked during a meeting with a financial professional and the benefit to you answering them honestly:

- *Where do you currently do your banking and why?*

    The reason for this question is to identify not only where but also why you chose to do business with a particular institution(s). According to your answers, based on the banker's knowledge of the competition, they may be able to inform you of the strengths of either that institution or why their institution fits you better. (Just a sidenote to any bankers reading this—do not trash the competition; it only makes you look bad to your customers.)

- *What type of deposit accounts do you have at other financial institutions, and what are the rates you earn on those relationships?*

    The answers to this question helps your banker identify if there is an opportunity to possibly get you a higher rate of return (i.e., make you more money) on the accounts that you have elsewhere. Everyone is looking for the best return, and if you have great relationships that are rewarding you and meeting your goals and objectives where you are already banking, then keep those accounts where they are. However, if you can receive a better return elsewhere, and you trust the banker and the institution, then take your money there.

- *What outstanding loan balances and interest rates do you have on your home mortgage, line(s) of credit, auto loan(s), student loan(s), personal loan(s), credit card(s), etc.?*

    We certainly find ourselves in a day where every little bit helps as it relates to saving money. These answers help your banker identify opportunities to lower your rates (i.e., save you money) by offering similar products that you currently have at a lower interest rate. This can be accomplished by transferring to new accounts or by combining some balances at an overall lower combined interest rate.

- *Where and what type of investment account relationships do you have?*

    Again, your banker is asking this question to find a way to earn you more money on the existing relationships that you currently have or to recommend putting together a plan for your financial future.

- *Who is your banker or financial adviser, and when was the last time you spoke or met with them?*

    Now more than ever, people need to meet with his or her financial guide whether it is a banker or financial adviser at least twice a year for a routine "financial checkup." This consistent practice ensures that everything is going according to plan and gives you the opportunity to address any changes that may have occurred since the last meeting.

If your banker/financial adviser is really doing a good job, then you should know his/her name, and be quite comfortable and willing to meet with them often to discuss your financial health. If you are not hearing from your banker/financial adviser or have no clue who they are, find one that you can trust, and establish a relationship. The same way that you know and trust your medical doctor is the same experience and relationship you deserve to have with your banker. No, it is not life or death but still very important.

Again, I want to help you understand that your banker is there to help you find your way or further assist you in accomplishing whatever is important to you financially. Great bankers and financial professionals do not and will not lead the way but rather follow your specific instructions and only make recommendations that meet and exceed your expectations.

The Branch Manager

When I reflect back on my years managing from directly within the branch, I smile because those were some of the most exciting and trying times of my career. Branch managers have the great responsibility of making sure that the entire branch is successful in all aspects—from personnel to customer service to sales. It is the responsibility of the branch manager to ensure that their employees are well trained, knowledgeable, courteous, professional, and productive. Branch managers are held accountable for the overall performance of the entire branch and are to ensure that all of the needs concerning customers and employees are addressed.

The benefit to you when a branch manager performs their job well is that all the functions of the branch are performing at optimum capacity. This simply means that when everyone within the branch is fulfilling his or her assigned responsibilities, the greatest beneficiary is you, the customer.

CHAPTER 5

The Banks' Purpose for the Accounts

While depositing your hard-earned money into the bank, have you ever asked yourself the question, What does the bank do with my money?

As we all know, businesses—especially banks—do not just offer products and services out of the goodness of their hearts but are looking to make a profit. The forthcoming chapters will further discuss many of the same types of accounts we have previously covered in order to give you a clear and detailed understanding of the various ways that "your money" makes the bank money.

Checking Accounts

Regardless of how you deposit funds into your account whether manually or electronically, the bank sincerely appreciates every penny and capitalizes on those funds. At the end of every day, the bank takes your funds and invests them into profitable vehicles for its own benefit (we will discuss this in greater detail later on in the book). The bank then earns a return on that investment and pays you a rate of interest on an annual basis, or what is referred to as the APY, as discussed in chapter 1.

Most checking accounts will pay you little to no interest because they typically have the most fluctuating balances. Because of this uncertainty, banks pay very little, if any, interest at all on the average balance maintained within the account (dividing the daily balance by the number of days within that month). Thus, enters the need for zero balance accounts and those that require low minimum balances.

Most people have checking accounts that do not require them to maintain a minimum balance. Now you may be thinking, *Well what is the problem with that? I can get all of my money if I want to at any time I want.* You are absolutely correct and do not have to worry about below minimum balance fees in this case. However, if you are an individual that does maintain a balance in your checking account of, let's say, $500 on average, but you keep it in a zero balance checking account, guess what? You are lending your $500 to the bank and not charging them any interest at all while they invest your money, earn a return, and pay you no interest on your money. Now just imagine what the bank is doing if you maintain an average account balance of $2,500 in your zero balance account. Yes, they are investing your money into investments that earn a return while again paying you zero ($0) dollars.

Think about this: on average, banks are not required to pay any interest at all on most consumer and business checking accounts, yet they earn upward of 4 percent on those balances. In addition, even on the accounts that require a minimum amount in order to earn interest, the bank still profits upward of 2.50 percent to 3 percent.

I want to clearly communicate to everyone reading this book that I am not telling you to pull all of your money out of the bank, and hide it under your mattress. I am just simply informing you of what is happening with your money when deposited in noninterest bearing accounts. You certainly benefit from the protection of your money being safe and insured by the bank. I just simply wish to explain how the bank profits using your money.

Financial institutions profit in a major way compared to how you benefit. I have already explained that banks pay minimal interest while earning at a premium, but please allow me to give you a clearer example of this fact.

Here is an example:

There are financial institutions that require anywhere from $15,000 up to $75,000 plus in deposits for their very best checking account in order for you to earn .01 percent (no that is not a typo) while the bank earns upward of 4 percent. Understanding this, let's do the math.

Your $15,000 x .001 APY = $15 interest paid to you

The bank using your same $15,000 x .04 APY = $600 the bank earns on your money

Just for the sake of examples, let's do the same using $75,000.

Your $75.000 x .001 APY = $75

The bank using your same $75,000 x .04 = $3,000

Hopefully, this shows you how the bank capitalizes on your money as it pertains to checking accounts.

Savings and Money Market Accounts

The savings account is established to help customers do just that—save money. Most times, this type of account will require a minimum balance in order to earn interest. The agreement between you and the bank is that you will always maintain a balance that the bank can count on being in your account, and in the event that you fall below the minimum balance, you will incur a fee (ballpark figure $20). Just as we did concerning checking accounts, let's look at what some banks' best savings accounts require and pay out to customers compared to what the bank earns on those same funds.

Here is an example:

You maintain $15,000 x .0010 APY = $15

The bank uses your $15,000 x .0275 APY = $412.50

Just for the sake of illustration, let's put in the really big numbers.

You maintain $1,000,000 X .0050 APY = $5,000

The bank uses your same $1,000,000 x .275 APY = $27,500

Need I say more? The bank is earning quite a hefty return compared to your return. Again, please understand that I am not saying that there is something wrong with the bank earning its money. I am just simply informing you of how they do it.

Loans

In the same manner that banks profit from the balances on your checking and savings accounts, they do the same when it comes to the balances that people carry on their loans. Banks can earn on average 1 percent on the outstanding balances of most consumer loans (mortgages, home equity loans and lines of credit, personal loans and lines of credit, auto loans, etc.)

When it comes to business loans (e.g., commercial loans, lines of credit, leases, etc.), banks can earn up to 2 percent. The reason that the rate of return is higher for business loans than consumer loans is simple—businesses generally carry larger balances.

Here is an example:

The bank takes the money in a checking account that has a minimum balance requirement, pays you 1 percent and lends that amount at, let's say, 7 percent. Well after the expenses of administering the transactions and paying the expense for having and maintaining the products—for this example, we'll say 1 percent. The bank will walk away with a 4 percent profit from the deposits, and 1 percent from the loans, for a profit of 5 percent. So although you are benefitting because your money is safe and secure while having the funds to make the purchases that you desire, the bank benefits from it all—keeping, lending, and investing your money.

What you need to know is that the bank takes the money that it has in deposits and lends that money out at a higher rate of interest, thus giving the bank in the above example a 4 percent rate of return.

The Truth about "Free Money" and the Attractive Advertising

Now that we have discussed the benefit of these accounts to the bank, please understand that banks need to raise deposits in order to lend money to the public. In plain English, in order for the bank to have, let's say, $10,000,000 in loans to customers, it must at the very least have $10,000,000 in deposits within the bank. At the end of every day, the bank must balance in the loan to deposit ratio, and when it doesn't, the bank must go to the federal government to borrow the money in order to make up the difference.

Here is an example:

Let's say that a small community bank had a hundred people come inside of the branch within one day and withdraw $5,000 each, totaling $500,000 in withdrawals. If at the end of that day the bank has $1,000,000 in outstanding loans, then it must then go to the federal government in order to borrow the deficiency of $500,000 at, let's say, a rate of 4 percent. It is certainly more expensive for banks to borrow from the federal government rather than you, the consumer, and/or businesses. Why? Because remember, for deposits, the bank generally pays zero to very little interest on those balances and lends at a premium, whereas, borrowing it from the government in order to maintain the loans established, and then having to pay that money back with interest, is not what the banks ever want to have to do. Knowing this, I will now explain to you why the sudden "attractive advertisements" show up offering high interest rates on deposits.

Have you ever visited your local branch and noticed a promotion advertising higher interest rates on an account you already have with the bank? I have witnessed people almost tumble over themselves from shock at the sudden rate change, almost as if to say, Whoa! Where did that come from?

Typically, after the customers gather themselves, they want to know how to get the same attractive rate offered on an account that I already have. Well, what do you think usually happens in this scenario? I'll tell you (as you already knew that I would). Most times the banker or manager has to explain to the customer that this higher interest rate is only available to either new accounts opened with the bank or existing customers adding new money from another institution into the bank.

Of course, this does not sit well with current customers that, in many cases, have had long-standing relationships with the bank prior to the new offer. Now I am not disputing the bank's ability to raise capital in order to operate and earn a profit. Again, I am simply explaining the process. When this occurs, existing customers are typically very frustrated, irritated, and feel unappreciated that new customers get an opportunity to benefit from the great promotion that existing customers cannot.

The truth of the matter is that the bank does not have to pay more for money that it already has, and further, it does not make good business sense to do so. Now this does open the door to the threat of losing existing customers with possible long-term relationships, but that is the bank's "risk versus reward" scenario. The bank is counting on an influx of new customers getting excited about the promotion and bringing over their new funds to earn that high interest rate as opposed to the possibility of losing existing customers.

The bank does all of this for a couple of reasons, but it all ties back to raising capital from the consumers and businesses through deposit acquisition rather than having to borrow from the federal government. Remember: regardless of the interest rate, the bank is going to earn a return on the balances. Even if the bank offers a very high rate of return that eats all of its profit and allows them to earn just 1 percent interest or simply break even, the ability to have deposits on hand to minimize the outstanding loan balances is much cheaper than the bank having to borrow the monetary difference from the federal government. Make sense? Hopefully so. This also applies to the bank's promotions that occasionally offer anywhere from $50 to $100 to open new checking accounts.

I hope that, by now, you clearly see that it is all about getting more money to invest and lend out at a premium while balancing the loan to deposit ratio. Yes, the bank may seemingly pay out a lot of money in order for money to come back in, but that is what any business does—they pay for the things (products) that will eventually bring in a positive return. If you notice, there is always an expiration date on these offers whether it be the interest rate or the "free money." Why? Because the bank only wants to attract enough funds to accomplish its priority, and it doesn't matter if it is to balance the loan portfolio or to increase deposits in order to be able to lend money—the attractive advertising benefits the bank far more than it does its customers.

CHAPTER 6

The Truth about "Convenience"

We talked about the many "conveniences" that financial institutions offer customers in order for them to have quick and easy access to their own cash. In this chapter, we will revisit some of those conveniences and systems that process the transactions of those products in order to show you how the bank benefits from them as well.

Checks

We all certainly understand why checks are necessary. They help alleviate the need to carry cash on our person while allowing us to make purchases, and pay bills. But how does the bank benefit from the convenience of writing checks, you ask? (Let me preface this by saying that the bank is not being sneaky in any regard to what I am about to tell you—just smart).

When you open a checking account, in most cases, you will receive your first order of checks for free. However, the bank makes money on every check order that you place. In this regard, bankers are encouraged to get you to upgrade to more personalized checks that fit your individuality, lifestyle, preferences, etc. There is certainly nothing at all wrong with that. I am just letting you know that every addition, every logo, and every specific text or quote that you want printed on your personal checks is driving revenue for the bank.

INSIDER INFORMATION

The average box of personalized checks cost you a ballpark figure amount of about $18. However, when or if you lose your checkbook or even just one check, it is going to cost you an average fee of $25 to stop payment on that check or series of checks. The stop payment fee is definitely worth the protection of keeping someone from getting their hands on your checking account information and performing unauthorized transactions on your account.

The challenge when writing checks is the fact that you must wait for the recipient to do his/her part by depositing it in a timely fashion. The timing of checks clearing the account is less of an issue for individuals who carry large balances. However, most people are watching their account balances like a hawk and are counting on transactions posting in a certain order to avoid the dreaded overdraft fee. When overdrafts occur, customers are charged a per item fee of typically $30 or more.

When you deal with checks, you are at the mercy of the holder of the check. While it certainly is the customer's responsibility to balance their checkbook every day to ensure that they have enough funds to cover their expenses, we all have had the "out of sight, out of mind" experience. Unfortunately, when this happens, we could face numerous overdraft fees because it only takes one forgotten transaction to throw everything out of whack.

ATM/Debit Cards

Just think back to the time when there were no ATM/debit cards, and you had no choice but to carry cash. You actually had a better sense of where you were in terms of your balance because as you made purchases, the funds in your pocket diminished. At some point, when you ran out of cash, you were automatically aware of how much money you had spent within a day because whatever you took from the bank had been depleted.

As fast-paced as the world is today, debit card usage is certainly keeping up with the speed of the day. That simple plastic card is used to process most personal and small business financial transactions. The fact that customers benefit from the debit card by not having to carry cash and having the ability to pay bills and make purchases is well understood. However, the transactions that most often overdraw checking accounts are those done with an ATM/debit card. Take a moment to count how many transactions in which you specifically used your ATM/debit card over a one-month period. If you are anything like me, the number of transactions performed with that little piece of plastic can be astounding.

How good are you at knowing, or even better, remembering, how much money you spend in one day using your debit card? Do you go home and enter into your checking account to register all of the transactions performed with your debit card? Probably not. (I know that there is probably someone saying, *Will, duh, there is online banking for that!* Well you are right, but online banking has its issues as well). With the ATM/debit card being used so often, there is always the potential of some transaction being forgotten and thus causing overdraft fees to be incurred.

The benefit to you in using your ATM/debit card is that most of your transactions should post to your account immediately and reflect on your online banking statement. However, not every purchase made with your ATM/debit card is posted right away, such as gasoline purchases. Have you ever noticed that? Why? Because gas stations only verify that you have at least one dollar available in your account and will allow you to fill up your entire car based on that verification. If you filled up your tank and actually spent (for example) $30, you may initially believe that everything is fine. Later on that day, or even the next day, you may see a posting on your account initially reflecting just one dollar spent, and if you do not pay close attention when balancing your account, you can potentially count that transaction as complete when it in fact is not. In this example, if you counted that dollar as the total purchase price and continued to use your debit card having forgotten about the other $29 pending to post to your account, you already know what is going to happen, don't you? You are going to incur a costly overdraft fee.

Things happen so fast when it comes to making purchases with your debit card, and the overdraft fees accumulate even faster when we miscalculate and forget about a purchase. Over the years, banks have made so much revenue from human error that the federal government had to step in to relieve people of the overdraft fee feast that banks were enjoying at the expense of hardworking American families. Further, most debit cards are linked to a checking account. So as discussed in chapter 5, the bank benefits from customers opening checking accounts in yet another way because they are counting on you to mess up in order to charge you their easy revenue generator—the overdraft fee.

Here is an example:

Imagine that one bank branch has 3,000 checking account customers. Now consider if just one-third of them (900 people) had just one overdraft fee of $35. Let's do the math.

900 x $35 = $31,500 in direct revenue for that one branch in just one day

Now we looked at a very conservative example, but, of course, we know that many will incur several overdraft fees because of multiple transactions posting. I also only used one branch in the example above, so let's look at how much the bank could potentially earn just from overdraft fees alone in one day because I just want to clearly illustrate how powerful the numbers are.

Below is an example:

You live in a major city, which has some of the largest financial institutions in the country. CGX Bank has seventy-five bank branches with an average of 2,000 checking account holders. Of the 2,000 checking account holders, 20 percent of them overdraw their account just one time at $35 within one day. Let's do the math.

75 x 400 x $35 = $1,050,000 in overdraft revenue in just one day

Pretty powerful and astounding numbers, which is one of the reasons banks gladly give you that convenient ATM/debit card in order for you to access your funds and very easily drive revenue for the bank. This does not include the revenue banks earn every time you swipe your card to make a purchase by charging that place of business a transaction fee. The bank truly profits on every side.

The Systems

Banks are ingenious when it comes to earning a profit at every opportunity even when it comes down to the systems that it uses to process your transactions. Many banks have figured out how to capitalize on how to process your transactions when they come into the bank. Many banks are going back to the way that it once was, and we will discuss that shortly. But let's begin with how a number of banks currently and will continue to process your transactions and benefit.

Today many banks receive your transactions within one day and process them by the end of that day. When they reconcile your account, many banks process all of your transactions from the largest to the smallest item regardless of the order in which the transactions actually posted to your account. As you knew that I would, I am going to plainly show you how the bank earns a ton of revenue with these processes in place.

Take this for example:

Let's say that you had a balance of $200 in your account that was available for use. Within that day, you had three checks post to your account in this order:

$25
$65
$145
$235 (total)

As we see, the checks posting in this order exceed the $200 balance, but the account should have enough to cover two of the checks and cause the customer to incur only one overdraft fee of $35. What the bank has figured out is how to maximize on this very simple process by posting items in the bank's best interest while "saying" that they are looking out for their customers' best interest, but that is not all together true.

This is what the bank does to capitalize on the same transactions posting.

Here is an example:

You had the same checks post to your account in the exact same order as above. The bank waits until the end of the day to process those same transactions, but they process them in order from the largest amount to the smallest.

$145
$65
<u>$25</u>
$235 (total)

As you see, when the bank processes your transactions in this order, only one check—the $145 item will be processed without a fee. The next largest check amount of $65 takes the account into the negative, followed by the $25 item, thus beginning the downward spiral into overdraft fees owed to the bank. But remember, that is not the actual order that the items came in. This is just how the bank chose to process the checks in order to gain instant revenue. In this example, the customer will incur two overdraft fees at $35 each ($7 total) as opposed to just one overdraft fee in the previous example using the same exact check amounts.

Banks have been capitalizing on this process for years, again producing immediate year over year revenue. Imagine how much money has been earned due to this process. In fact, banks have benefitted so much that the government recently intervened and forced them to go back to processing transactions in the exact order that they come in.

Overall, the reason for so many convenience products is to make it very inconvenient for customers to ever want to leave the bank they are with. Consider this—the bank understands that the more convenience products that you have with them, the less likely you are to leave even if you are unhappy. The banks actually refer to convenience products as "sticky products." Why? Because that is exactly what the outcome typically is—customers stick with the same bank even when dissatisfied. It seems to be too much of a hassle to reopen all of these same products and services elsewhere (e.g., automatic withdrawals, direct deposit, debit card, etc.) and then redirect all of your financial obligations to a new account number rather than just stay put and accept the level of service you are receiving.

Do not get me wrong. There are many financial institutions that really do care about providing excellent customer service whether you believe that or not. I have worked for a few of them in the past. However, banks know that there will be mistakes as it relates to some service failure whether by employees, products, services, or systems. Their fail-safe plan is to have customers own as many products as possible, so that they stick with them through all of the ups and downs.

CHAPTER 7

The Truth about Loans

The banks' profits from loan products align pretty much the same way as deposits do, concerning advertising and revenue generated from the spread and fee returns.

Banks need to lend money for a number of reasons:

1. When there are more deposits on hand than loans, the ratio needs to balance out.
2. A bank's strength is greatly determined by the number and dollar amount of outstanding loans it has in good standing.
3. Banks earn significant revenue from new loan balances acquired from competitor banks.

So just like the fantastic advertisements that you occasionally see promoting new consumer accounts and high interest rates for deposits, the bank does the same for its loan products with the same outcome in mind—revenue.

When you hear about lower rates being offered than what you currently receive, you should certainly inquire to see if there is an opportunity for you to cash in and save money on your current loan obligations. What you have to do is, make sure that refinancing your loans will be worth it in the end. There are a number of things to consider before doing this, but here are a few:

1. Am I comparing apples with apples? Meaning, how does the loan I am considering match up to what I already have?
2. Am I truly going to save money for the same, shorter-, or longer-term?
3. Are there any other requirements that I must complete in order to get the advertised rate (such as open an additional account)?

Many times the interest rate alone is not a reason to consider whether to refinance current outstanding balances owed on existing loans. In fact, rates should actually be one of the last things that you consider before getting a loan, in my opinion. The reason is, because for the most part, interest rates are going to be what they are, and banks come pretty close to each other in the end. Very rarely do you find one bank completely blowing the competition out of the water as it pertains to interest rates. If you happen to find yourself in this scenario, remember that there is always a reason behind one bank being significantly lower with rates than most.

As a banker and manager, I worked for many financial institutions that did not necessarily want or need to have the "best rate." When I really understood how to truly *help* clients, I performed full assessments of their needs and would look for all of the possibilities to roll other higher rate loans into one. The rate may not have been the best for the one product, however, when you included other current outstanding debt at significantly higher interest rates than that which the bank offered, many times it made sense to roll as many outstanding debts into one overall cheaper rate loan. Rates are just the "teaser" to pique your interest.

You must always keep in mind that banks are looking to make "new money" as it relates to loans. This is the reason why many banks will not refinance their existing loan balances to lower amounts. Again, in business, I do not disagree with that. Place yourself in the banks' position.

INSIDER INFORMATION

Here is an example:

If you established with a customer a home equity loan for $100,000 at 7 percent interest and wanted to advertise that you were now lending home equity loans at 4 percent, you would certainly attract new business. But you would also have to know that as soon as your existing customer receives word of such a great offer, they are going to make a beeline to you to refinance their current existing loan at the lower interest rate. If you refinanced the remaining existing balance at a lower rate, you would then be in a business sense, hurting your own self.

This is why banks will many times require that in order for a customer to receive the lower rate, they will have to increase their existing loan amount by a certain dollar amount. For example, maybe $25,000. By doing this, the bank is able to maintain its revenue in the long run because of the additional loan balance and term that has been added to the loan even though the rate is now lower. Make sense?

So in the bank's defense, they must make decisions that also take into consideration their own best interest. The bank understands that the refusal to negotiate refinancing existing loan balances, unless they increase their current loan, may cause customers to look elsewhere to refinance their loans. The bank also takes into consideration that those customers who also have deposit and investment relationships may very well close out those accounts as well. Again, this is the bank's confidence in the risk versus reward theory that they will gain more new customers and new relationships from competitor banks than the number of existing customers that will ultimately leave.

When considering taking advantage of what appears to be attractive offers to establish new loan relationships with banks compared to what you already have, you must read all of the fine print, and educate yourself to the "rules of the game." You must find out the consequences to all of the "ifs:"

- What am I going to have to pay in upfront fees "if" I decide to agree to the terms of this loan?
- What happens to the rate "if" I have a late payment?

- What happens "if" I pay this loan off earlier than the agreed-upon terms?

The truth of the matter is that many times people are applying for loans just based on the emotional reaction to seeing such attractive offers without taking into account all of the things mentioned above. The emotional purchase drives revenue in so many ways, not just for banks but any industry. But remember this: regardless of what industry people make their emotional purchases in, they all have to "bank" somewhere with their deposits and loan relationships. The bank capitalizes on every point.

As it pertains to *upfront fees*, banks will often require that a customer pay for different administrative items in order for the loan application to be processed and before the loan is finally approved such as application fees, appraisal fees (concerning home loans), down payments, closing costs, etc.

Concerning *late payments*, the bank will not only charge a late payment fee, but some also will increase the rate on your loan if such a thing were to happen. I have known of banks or finance companies that have gone so far as to double the rate on current loans when the bank receives a late payment from a customer. Also, concerning rate increases on loans (just as a sidenote), customers should find out if the rate being advertised is just an introductory rate that will, at some later point in time, increase to some predetermined amount or if the rate being offered will be permanent throughout the life of the loan.

Early pre-payment penalties can add up to being quite expensive as well. While being able to pay off a loan and getting rid of additional debt earlier than agreed upon is an advantage to the customer. You should certainly know that the bank, in many instances, is not going to allow you to just leave that easily. I, again, do not disagree with the bank in holding customers to the agreed-upon terms of the loan that they have entered into, but customers need to understand exactly what they are getting into.

In the event of an early loan payoff, some banks require that a certain percentage of the outstanding balance be paid along with an additional fee, which could consist of a certain percentage of the credit limit or a predetermined maximum amount, whichever number is of greater benefit to the bank.

You must understand that the bank has already counted on the interest that it expects to receive over the life of the loan it establishes with you. The bank has already forecasted future revenues based on the agreed-upon terms of the loan, and when a customer alters that plan by paying the loan off early, the bank then makes up for its loss by charging these types of fees.

At some point in life, we all will most likely need to establish a loan with a bank, and that is certainly not a bad thing. It is the responsibility of every individual to do his or her own due diligence prior to agreeing to the loan's terms. Throughout my banking career, I had many unfortunate conversations with customers that had established long-term loans without fully understanding all of the requirements. It certainly is not a fun conversation to have with a customer after they recognize that what they thought they were getting in reality is not what they have.

If you have questions, do not be afraid to ask. Ask as many questions as you feel necessary in order to make an educated decision about your finances. If you do not ask, you leave yourself open to the advantage of the bank.

CHAPTER 8

What's Really Motivating the Bankers, Tellers, and Managers

Money is a great motivator regardless of the industry in which one works. There is nothing wrong with that, at all, as far as I see. Earning money is how we provide for our families and ourselves. It is how we plan for the future of our children and retirement. It is how we survive.

We all would like to believe that employees within the banking/financial industry do what they do simply because they enjoy helping people, and in many cases, this is the motivation behind bankers taking extremely great care of their customers. However, this line of work also offers a great opportunity for increased compensation.

To the many branch managers, bankers, financial advisers, and tellers reading this book, please know that I have a great appreciation for what it is that you all do on a daily basis. You deal with two of the most important things on the planet—people and their money. You do not have an easy job, and I know this firsthand. I applaud those who take what they do seriously enough to have integrity in their profession and look for every opportunity to really help people achieve financial success.

Bankers

Bankers are self-driven, money-motivated individuals who understand that their earning potential stems from commissions. Therefore, what banks have done is cap their base salary, allowing bankers just enough money to survive but not enough to thrive. Because of this, bankers must proactively look for every opportunity to assist customers in exchange for a chance to raise their earning potential. Additionally, there is usually a monetary benefit for those who refer business to the bank and close deals.

I have managed hundreds of financial professionals throughout my career. When I asked employees why he/she chose to work in banking, the one answer received most often was, "Because I like to help people." I would always think to myself, *Wow that is great!* However, many times I came to discover that answer was not always completely honest. To be clear, what I recognized was

- some thought that "helping" meant that they simply did what the customer told them to do,
- some thought that "helping" meant that they only needed to be nice and polite to customers, and
- some thought that because they knew personal things such as children and pet names that they really knew their customers.

I also realized that the advice some bankers offered really was not helpful at all. Financial professionals (e.g., managers, bankers, financial advisers, etc.) should take the necessary steps to identify every opportunity to save or make their customers money. That means, they need to ask the necessary questions to ensure that a customer does not walk out of the bank with only partial help. I'll give you an example.

Here is an example:

A banker has an appointment to discuss investments that the customer has at other institutions. The banker has no problem asking all of the necessary questions in order to make the best recommendation to help the customer meet his/her financial objectives because investments are his/her strength. However, the banker never asks about the customer's current outstanding loans because the banker is not all that comfortable talking about loans or even worse, just does not care because, in their opinion, loans do not pay enough commission.

The customer leaves with a great investment recommendation but has only been partially helped. Why? Because the banker did not discuss the high interest rate loans that the customer continues to carry. If the banker really wanted to help, he/she could have investigated refinancing those high interest rate loans at lower rates, thus helping the customer add the additional funds saved from the loan into their investments.

Because of this type of behavior, banks have things in place to help motivate their employees to take a proactive approach to meeting their customers' needs. Many financial institutions (and any sales industry actually) have sales campaigns and incentives in order to drive results that ultimately affect producing revenue for the bank.

To the bank customers reading this—please do not assume that the financial professionals within your local bank only offer certain products and services in order to capitalize on you. Yes, those financial professionals usually receive additional compensation when you accept the products and services that the bank offers. There is nothing wrong with this practice at all. Actually, it is a just reward for a job well done, especially if the recommendation saves or makes you money.

However, you should be suspicious when the product or service being offered just does not make good common or financial sense. This is why I always urge customers to bank with highly recommended and trusted professionals. If you end up meeting with someone that you are unfamiliar with, ask the necessary questions in order to assure yourself that the banking professional has your best interests in mind. If you are not comfortable with that person for any reason, keep searching for the right person until you are satisfied.

For many bankers, there is an excellent opportunity to make a lot of money for properly taking care of customers. When done correctly, and with the customers' best interest in mind, a banker positions himself/herself to benefit greatly for a job well done.

Most financial institutions compensate bankers for every product and service that they successfully get a customer to accept. Typically, when a banker hits a certain threshold of "points" that are directly aligned with the products and services offered by the bank, they begin to cash in and qualify for additional commissions and recognition. In short, the more products and services bankers sell, the more money they can potentially earn. This also benefits you, the customer, because the more opportunities a banker finds to save you money by lowering high debt, or to make you money by offering products that put more money in your wallet, the more money the banker makes. Sounds like a great trade off, if you ask me.

Bankers who really help customers with their finances will find success and enjoy the privilege of being recognized as the best in the country. In addition, they are eligible to enjoy all-expense-paid trips to five star resorts and rewards such as luxury vehicles leased at the bank's expense.

When I trained financial professionals on how to effectively serve customers, there was nothing like the reward of seeing them honored as the best of the best. I always encouraged bankers to offer only those products and services that benefit the customer and never to offer products that would not. I also strongly advised that bankers listen to what their customers tell them, as well as what they are *not* saying, and then make recommendations that not only meet but also exceed their expectations. Specifics of those recommendations can be found in my book, *Listen If You Want To Succeed!*

However, remember that if the threshold set by the bank for the bankers to exceed is not met, then the banker has nothing to benefit from. I hope that this will motivate bankers and financial professionals to do all that they can to help people with their finances at every opportunity.

Tellers

For tellers, some banks establish minimum referral goals and customer service satisfaction scores in order for them to receive additional incentives or pay. So in essence, the bank expects tellers to identify a certain number of needs and refer enough customers over to the bankers that will, again, drive revenue. The teller receives compensation for every referral that ends with the sale of a product or service. Those successful referrals equal more money, recognition, gifts, and, in some cases, trips, which tellers can enjoy. Since tellers are considered the "face" of any bank, in my humble opinion, this is a great incentive since they interact with more customers than any other bank employee does.

Managers

The branch manager has the responsibility of making sure that the bankers are successfully offering and selling customers as many appropriate products and services as they can. In doing so, the banker is meeting, and hopefully exceeding, the needs of their customers while, at the same time, earning more money and enjoying their career. The branch manager also has to make sure that the tellers are providing the level of service expected and identifying customers to refer to the bankers in order for them to receive teller referral credit, which allows them to earn extra compensation.

To keep the branch manager focused on driving revenue, some banks have campaigns and competitions throughout the year in order to push for year-to-year growth in revenue, products, and services offered. As in any business, a sufficient goal to shoot for is about 10 percent in revenue and sales. Banks will provide the branch managers with their sales results and increase that number by that 10 percent.

Below is an example:

If a branch opened a hundred checking accounts during the months of January to March of the previous year, then the goal for the same period of the current year would be to open 110 checking accounts. The same goes for any other products offered by the bank such as credit cards, loans, investments, etc.

The branch manager must figure out and devise a strategy as to how they are going to engage everyone within their team to grow the business. Successfully doing so and meeting the goals given by the bank, qualifies the branch manager to enjoy the benefits of recognition (depending on where they rank with their peers based on who performed the best) by receiving nice commission payouts on a quarterly or annual basis depending on the bank. At the end of the year, the best of the best managers are also rewarded with all-expense-paid trips to five star resorts where they can bring along a guest. Depending on the bank, the very elite managers receive wonderful gifts, money, etc., along with the trip.

At the end of the day, it is the responsibility of the branch manager to make sure the bank is profitable. Along with driving revenue via sales and the products and services provided, the manager also has to ensure that the bank is operationally sound. Managers are ultimately responsible for all losses incurred and must do everything within their power to limit risk to the bank. This realm of responsibility is so important because any sales revenue generated can be undermined by losses incurred due to just one banker who does not follow specific instructions that limit fraud or one teller who does not take the appropriate steps when making deposits or cashing checks.

Branch managers, bankers, and tellers are the driving forces to the overall success of any bank. Financial institutions recognize this and understand that in order to get more results, they have to count on these individuals to get the job done, and compensate them for their efforts. Those who do their job the right way certainly deserve every dollar earned and every gift received. Congratulations to the best of the best in the banking/financial services industry who serve their customers with integrity!

CHAPTER 9

The Pressure to Impress Wall Street

When financial institutions fail, so does our economy.

Every bank has an ultimate goal in mind when it comes to their performance, and that goal is to receive a passing grade from Wall Street. Without Wall Street's blessing, the bank is a sitting duck. When banks perform well, the economy gets a boost as it relates to the Dow Jones, NASDAQ, etc. This allows banks to receive a "thumbs-up" from Wall Street that then encourages investors to go ahead and invest their money into the financial institutions. And what does that mean for banks? More revenue of course!

Consider this: every business in the country has to bank somewhere, correct? Yes. Banks forecast their expectations of future quarterly results to Wall Street, and when the bank meets or exceeds their predictions, they receive Wall Street's blessing. But when they fall short of their predictions, into the doghouse they go, which means that the public's confidence in that financial institution weakens, which threatens a loss of revenue.

Remember in chapter 5 when we discussed how the banks benefit when deposits are made, and loans are established? The returns are even larger when it comes to business accounts and loans because they generally carry larger balances, which convert into higher revenue for the banks to profit from. When you add up all of the deposits and loans of a bank, this, in many ways, reflects the financial report card of businesses and the consumers that bank with that institution.

INSIDER INFORMATION

Everything starts and stops with the bank, and again, we must understand that there is a trickle-down effect when banks do not perform well. When deposit balances go down because businesses are not earning as much as a result of consumers not buying their products, banks do not earn the returns that they would expect on those deposits. The same applies when business and consumer loans go into default or get charged off (i.e., unpaid loans by the borrower that the bank counts as a loss). The reason(s) for the decrease in loan and deposit balances has an inverse reaction regarding how it directly affects the bank.

When consumers find themselves overextended and in debt because "when the getting was good," banks were establishing loans (that they should not have) with consumers that could not afford to repay them. Those consumers, at some point, stopped making payments. Because banks were approving no document loans, not requiring money down, and even approving loans that were not A-paper loans (i.e., loans that would normally be turned down based on the standard criteria) and approved them in the subprime market for the sake of chasing dollars, this is what happens. It certainly did not help when greedy real estate people were manipulating the numbers and selling homes at inflated prices to consumers while the bank was approving those loans as well.

When consumers were unable to maintain those mortgages, the rug was pulled out from under the banks, and they took major hits to their loan portfolios. Allow me to paint a very clear picture for you.

Here is an example:

Let's just say that ten different banks within your city had twenty customers, each that fit the above description of a consumer during the mortgage foreclosure crisis. If each of those mortgage balances equaled $200,000, this alone represents a major negative impact on these financial institutions. Let's do the math:

Ten banks x twenty customers = 200 customers
200 customers x $200,000 = $40,000,000 in loan foreclosures balances

We will not even begin to calculate the amount of interest the bank lost. I changed my mind—let's calculate the loss of interest to the bank:

$40,000,000 x 7.25 percent over 30 years = $58,233,384.33

Wow! That is astounding, especially considering that we used conservative figures.

When banks begin taking large losses in its loan portfolio, they have to replace those losses with profits earned that may have been placed into what some refer to as their loan loss reserves (i.e., a savings account from their profits specifically kept to make up for loan losses). Yes, the banks have to save for rainy days as well. And what the bank has come to learn is that when it rains, it really pours.

Further, everything that goes on with businesses and consumers directly affects the financial world. When jobs were lost at rapid rates due to company downsizing, relocating, and outsourcing, fewer dollars were earned by consumers. Because of this, fewer dollars were deposited into banks, loans began to go into default, fewer dollars were being spent with businesses, etc. Moreover, when consumers are earning less money while their debt continues to rise, they personally suffer major losses, and inevitably, so does the bank.

The downward spiral continues when consumers and businesses begin to stop making their loan payments on time due to lack of money to meet their obligations, and their credit score pays the price. Simply put, banks are not going to lend money to people whose credit is bad, which means any opportunity for establishing new loans at lower interest rates is lost. However, that does not stop the bank from focusing on meeting its goal of making a good impression on Wall Street. Why? Because they have so much riding on the performance grading that they receive from them.

Unfortunately, that means the pressure mounts…breathing down the necks of those that work for the bank to perform fast. The CEO has missions and objectives that he/she would like to accomplish but receive a great deal of instructions from the financial institution's board of directors as well. The CEO then meets with the bank's top executives who provide leadership to the different levels of businesses and map out their strategic plan of what they feel is necessary to focus on.

At the banks I worked for, I found that the CEOs who provided leadership were pretty awesome individuals with an exceptional ability to communicate their message and vision while motivating their employees to take personal ownership to perform and deliver results. They had a gift for instilling company pride within their employees, but it always amazed me how different the message became as it was passed down from level to level and how less motivating, more threatening, and full of fear for lack of performance it contained.

I have sat in meetings with the CEO and top-level leadership of the bank at conferences held out of town to discuss issues, plans, and expectations. I would listen to every word that the CEO spoke and was fired up to get the job done. However, by the time I arrived back home, whether in a meeting or on a conference call, the communication's original tone had drastically changed. I sometimes wondered if I missed another meeting held after the one that I had just attended that relayed a completely different message. All I knew was that the message somehow lost the positive sentiment it originally embodied as it traveled downstream.

Next comes the pressure for financial professionals to perform and immediately produce results. Large goals begin to come from out of nowhere with time lines that no one was expecting. I clearly understand that, in business, last minute adjustments must sometimes be made, and desperate times certainly do call for desperate measures. However, there is a right way to get the job done and a wrong way. Unfortunately, in many instances, the wrong way is the method of choice to meet the demands of the bank in order to, again, impress Wall Street.

Are you able to guess who feels the most pressure? It is the people that are on the front lines servicing customers within the branches and offices of the bank. Sometimes the pressure can be so heavy for people to perform that. Those who have flourished and thrived in their career in the past, find themselves questioning their abilities that have brought them success for years. This does not mean that fresh, new approaches should not replace outdated, obsolete ways of doing business, or that goals should not increase. But it certainly does not help the financial professionals to meet or exceed the heavy expectations of the bank when the economy is struggling, and people are losing their jobs and having their credit negatively impacted.

As stated in chapter 5, loan and deposit balances drive a great deal of revenue for banks. But when it comes to bankers trying to identify loan opportunities if the customer's credit is bad because of late payments, charge offs, etc. due to the loss of a job, the banker's hands are tied. In addition, when funds are low due to no income, you can count on deposit balances diminishing. This translates into a challenge for bankers to identify deposit relationships and balances at other banks that may not pay as high an interest rate. I recognize that this does not apply to every individual in the world, and despite the economy and unemployment, there are millions of people that have weathered the storm with little to no negative impact to their finances and/or credit. However, the sensationalizing by the media of those negative conditions many times drives fear for people to do nothing concerning their financial conditions even when it makes sense for them to do so.

This certainly does not stop the bank from expecting their employees to produce results in order to meet its objective—Wall Street's approval. Therefore, marching orders go out to immediately open accounts, identify money in deposits and investments, and try to get as many loan applications approved as possible. That is fine, but when the underlying tone is *do it or else*, the same employees that successfully helped customers naturally are now forced into a robotic mode of moving units for the sake of producing numbers without providing the quality professionalism and service that the customer really deserves. When this process rears its ugly head, you soon find bank employees, at times, feeling forced between a rock and a very hard place.

All for the sake of producing numbers, financial professionals have been faced with making the unfortunate decision of compromising what they know to be the best thing to do for a customer. I have worked for a number of different banks and have always expressed to those that I have had the privilege of leading and managing to always do what they know to be right and best on behalf of their customer. Nevertheless, when the hammer comes down from above to get numbers, I have witnessed bankers do unethical things to produce immediate results for the sake of getting upper management off their backs. But this decision, at some point, will come back and possibly cause some type of disciplinary action up to and including termination of employment.

Here is an example:

Let's say that the bank is making a strong push for new checking accounts because they feel that it is not opening enough. A banker may have a customer who actually wants to open a savings account, but because the banker feels pressured to get checking accounts, he/she may tell the customer that they are opening a savings account, but it is actually a checking account. At some point, when the customer finds out what happened, they come back to the bank angry and confused as to how something like this could happen. The banker, knowing what really happened and why, acts surprised and finds him/herself awkwardly trying to explain the situation.

or

The bank wants a push on credit cards, so the pressure comes down to produce results. The banker assists a customer who is opening up new accounts and finds she/he has been preapproved for the bank's credit card. After trying to get the customer to see the benefits of accepting the credit card, the customer declines. Well I have witnessed situations where the banker still approves the customer for the credit card and has it sent out to them. The banker knows that when the customer receives the card, they will receive a nasty call about it. The banker tells the customer something like, "I thought that you said yes to the offer" or "There must be some mistake. If you don't want the card, then simply call, and cancel the card." These are just a few examples of what bank pressure can do to its employees in order to meet Wall Street's expectations.

The individuals that give in to the pressure of doing whatever it takes to hit today's numbers eventually end up forfeiting their future with the bank. It certainly is not worth jeopardizing your career and not being able to provide for your family. However, the way it is presented can make some believe that they have no other choice. And for those that are able to withstand the pressure, do it the right way and still manage to produce. It never seems to be enough. In many regards, the bank paints a "What have you done for me lately (meaning today)" attitude. Every day is not going to be great, and actually some will be seemingly unproductive, but there are always days of prosperity too.

I do not condone slackers and those that look for every opportunity not to produce and drive revenue for the bank the right way while earning more money for themselves. That is a whole other issue that needs to be addressed to get those individuals into either a better fitting role or maybe even career. I am an advocate for the hardworking professionals within the industry that fall victim to the challenges beyond their control. However, their feet are held to the fire as if it is their fault.

What you should know is that acquisition of new accounts and loans represent future forecasted earnings for the bank. It is very important that a bank continue to reflect growth in the number of household relationships that it has. When it does not appear that way, the bank gets in trouble with big brother Wall Street and will not receive the stamp of approval it desires and needs.

CHAPTER 10

Who It's Really about—
the Shareholders

If by now you do not understand, the bank makes money all the time. There is nothing that we can do about changing how banks earn their profits because, again, they do provide products and services that every consumer and business needs. Nevertheless, we can educate ourselves so that we may capitalize as well.

There are only two ways that banks make their money: via deposit spread and/or fees. We have discussed both of these methods extensively throughout this book. Now we will look at what the banks' strategy becomes when these two revenue sources are challenged.

Regarding the deposit spread, remember: the more accounts opened that maintain balances (specifically ones that do not require any interest be paid out such as consumer and business accounts), the more the bank profits. The bank is always looking for an opportunity to make money off your money, never allowing money holds to remain in cash accounts where it earns no return. Therefore, the bank is always investing your money into either treasuries or loans in order to receive interest and a return.

However, the bank shares a part of its return with holders who collect interest on their accounts. Therefore, maintaining large amounts of money in a bank where you can collect a return is a benefit for you. Again, this is why you need a trusted financial adviser to point you in the direction that you desire to go financially. Creating a strategic plan will allow you to capitalize on the returns you are looking for.

Understand that in times like these when people are struggling to find jobs and are strapped for cash, the balances within accounts begin to deplete, thus affecting the bank's return on those balances. When the deposit spread is heavily affected, the only other place for the bank to make up ground and still make a profit is in the fees assessed to account holders for either violation of some account agreement or requirement in order to maintain the product or service that the customer has.

Let's look at some of the fees that banks charge customers:

- annual fees (loans, mortgages, and credit cards)
- overdraft fees
- below minimum balance fees
- check order fees
- money order / cashier check fees
- check stop payment fees
- return check item fees
- foreign ATM fees
- wire transfer fees
- statement copy fees

These fees make up for the shortfall and many times is what brings financial institutions the profits that they enjoy. I am not saying that bank customers should not have to pay for the services that they need or for not maintaining the agreement established with the bank, I am just educating every reader to the many fees associated with the bank.

Because these fees are a very important part of how the bank makes its money, this is why there is very little tolerance for reversing fees once they are assessed to a customer. In most cases, when a customer requests consideration to possibly reverse any fee incurred, the decision maker has to take into account a number of things. Let's review a few of them:

- How long have you been a customer?
- How many times has this occurrence happened in the past?
- What is the potential loss in revenue to the bank in reversing this fee?
- What are your total relationships with the bank?

Why are these some of the questions asked? Simple. There must be a determination as to how profitable you are to the bank—is this an isolated incident, and why should the bank return this fee? The bank is *always* going to do what is in its own best interest. Banks have gone so far as to predetermine how much a customer is eligible to receive in fee refunds, if the need arises. Remember: it is the responsibility of the customer to keep their accounts in good standing. There is no getting around that. The moment your accounts are not in good standing for whatever reason, the fees are coming. Moreover, if you happen to cross the threshold of mercy that the bank allows, there is a great chance that you will not receive any of those fees back.

The branch managers and decision makers of the bank have the responsibility of monitoring and managing the reversal of the fees assessed and reversed for customers. Managers have the hefty responsibility of ensuring that the bank is profitable overall, and if the sales needed are not accomplishing the goal, fees become one of the areas for the bank to capitalize on. Consider this: when a customer is guilty of not honoring the agreed-upon terms of maintaining their account, that fee assessed is considered free money to the bank. The bank knows that the customer is more than likely going to bring that account into good standing by paying the fee and placing the money needed to back into the account. In the case where a customer overdraws the account and allows it to remain negative to the point that the bank wants to close out the account, the bank simply reports the negative account to the credit bureaus thus hindering the customer in most cases from being able to bank somewhere else. In short, the bank wins either by the customer satisfying the account or by charging the account off at as minimal a loss as possible.

Throughout my fifteen-year banking career, I personally took pride in knowing that I meant exactly what I said to customers every time that I told them that I am going to look for every opportunity to make or save you money. It was my mission and goal with every customer and client to only make recommendations that made sense. I was not going to product push just for the sake of hitting numbers or make decisions that did not make sense to do on behalf of customers.

The bank certainly promotes uncovering every opportunity to reduce a customer's debt through offering lower rate loans, as well as identifying all relationships at other financial institutions to pay a higher return on those funds. But at the end of the day, whether it was a loan approved and advanced, a deposit or investment brought into the bank from a competitor, or a fee assessed to a customer, it is all about the revenue generated in order to drive profit for the bank and a return on the investment of the shareholder.

That is who it is really all about—the bank's shareholders. Not that it is a bad thing to benefit those who have the confidence to invest into financial institutions. But those that run the bank at the expense of its employees, solely in the name of satisfying shareholders, many times cross a fine line. There are thousands of unmotivated conference calls and humiliating meetings that many managers and bankers find themselves becoming a part of for not accomplishing the bank's expectations. In the case of people just being underperformers, yes, they may need to hear it from time to time about the need to strategize and come up with not only a plan to succeed, but also how to execute that plan.

Currently, for the most part, every bank is struggling, and those that are successful are not doing it at the level that would like simply because all banks, even the good ones, are guilty by association. Those bank employees that take pride in what they do professionally and give it their all every day but still seem to come up short, unfortunately, pay a heavy price of working under extreme pressure, anxiety, fear, intimidation, threats, and duress—all for the sake of the bank wanting to perform ultimately just for the shareholders to benefit.

It is my hope that the banking world will learn from its past mistakes, which have brought it to where it is today. With the right leadership and truly doing what is in the very best interest of its customers and clients while taking care of and showing loyalty to its faithful employees—especially in the down times—things can turn around.

What you, the customer, and clients should clearly know is that you and your money are much more powerful than you realize. *The bank can earn nothing without your money.* In fact, we have witnessed the power of your money in that over a hundred banks have failed since 2009. When consumers and businesses lose confidence in the strength of a bank and begin to withdraw their money, the bank has to do something drastic in order to turn things around. When they do not, the government steps in and identifies another bank to take over in order to salvage as much as possible. Have you heard of any banks all of a sudden having a "name change" lately? Yes, it is true. You have more power than you know!

ABOUT THE AUTHOR

William A. Eaddy II is a recognized leader in every industry that he engages, including banking, investments, nonprofit, city and county government, entertainment, hotel and restaurant, and religious. Eaddy has over twenty-five years of executive leadership and management experience and credits all of his success to his faith in God and his parents Dr. Michael and Lady Christine "Rose" Eaddy. He started his illustrious banking career and climbed the corporate ladder, beginning his career as a young nineteen-year-old peak-time coin teller working fifteen hours per week to ten years later, being one of the youngest first vice presidents and retail district managers in the country for JP Morgan Chase, overseeing thirteen bank branches, hundreds of employees, and managing over a billion dollars in relationships. Eaddy was recognized by JP Morgan Chase as one of its top 10 percent managers and leaders in their entire retail banking organization in the world. Eaddy went on to become vice president and retail district manager of every US Bank location within the city of Chicago and its immediate surrounding suburbs. They are twelve in total. At US Bank, he was again a recognized leader in sales, service, and management, featured and celebrated around the country for his phenomenal ability to lead, motivate, show the way, and hold accountable those who reported to him within his organization.

He has been a licensed financial adviser, licensed real estate broker, licensed insurance agent and more. Eaddy was born and raised in the city of Chicago and advocates and educates the communities in which he resides and serves. He is a proud father of two beautiful daughters.

Printed in the USA
CPSIA information can be obtained
at www.ICGtesting.com
CBHW061717141124
17318CB00019B/495

9 781646 282074